Butterfly Coloring Book For Adults

An Adult Coloring Book of 40 Detailed and Patterned Butterflies by a Variety of Artists

Adult Coloring World

ISBN-13: 978-1523252985
ISBN-10: 1523252987

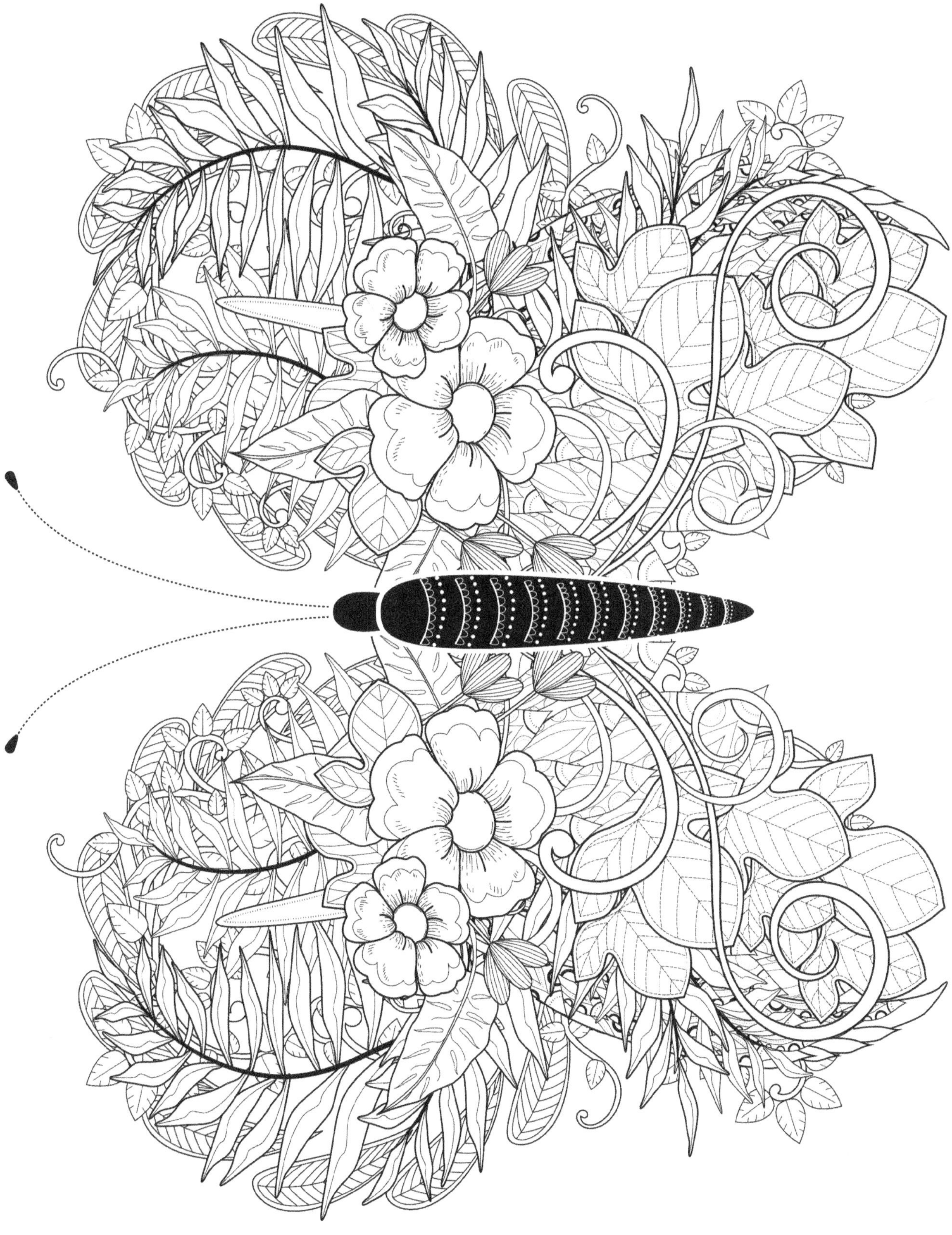

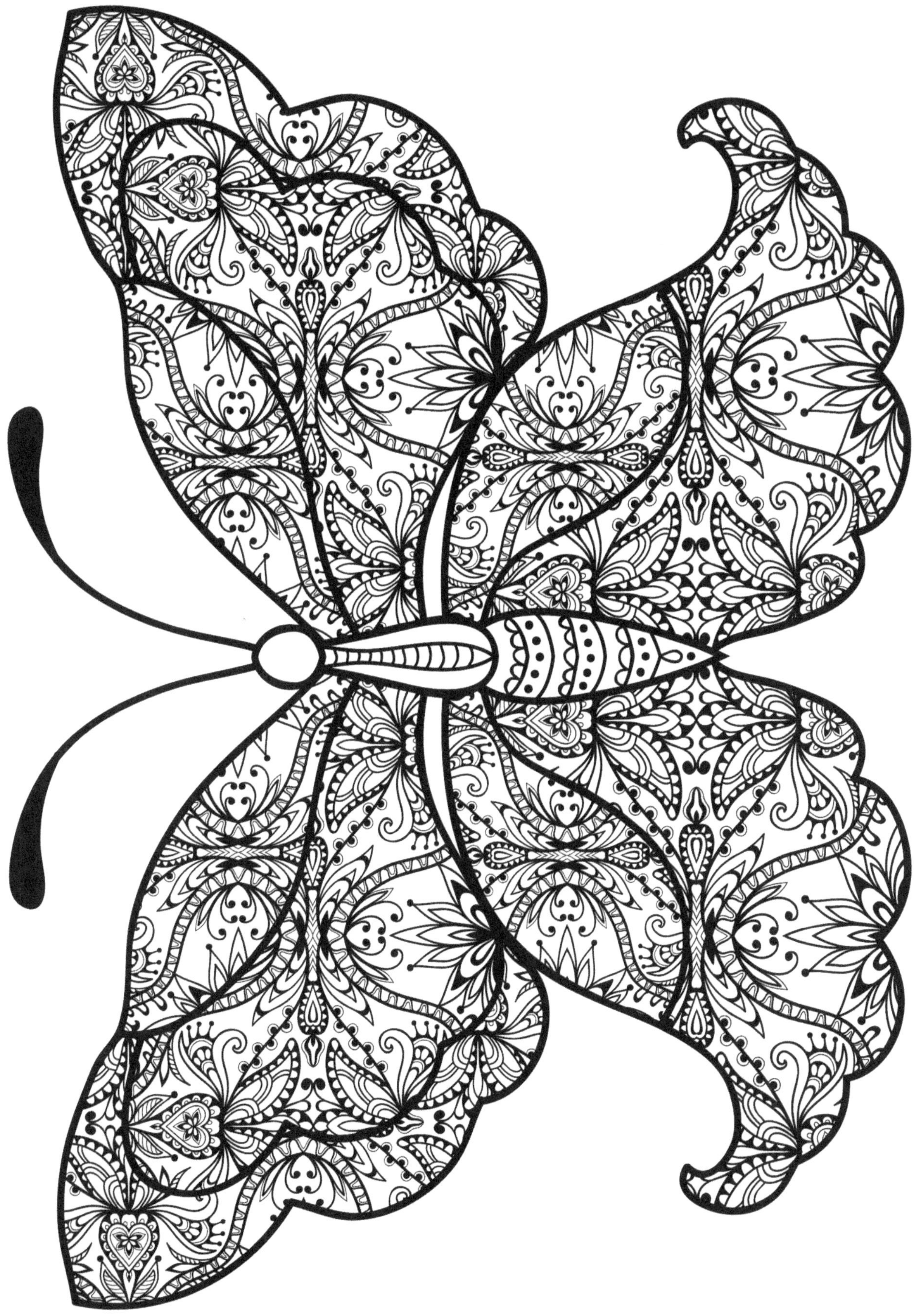

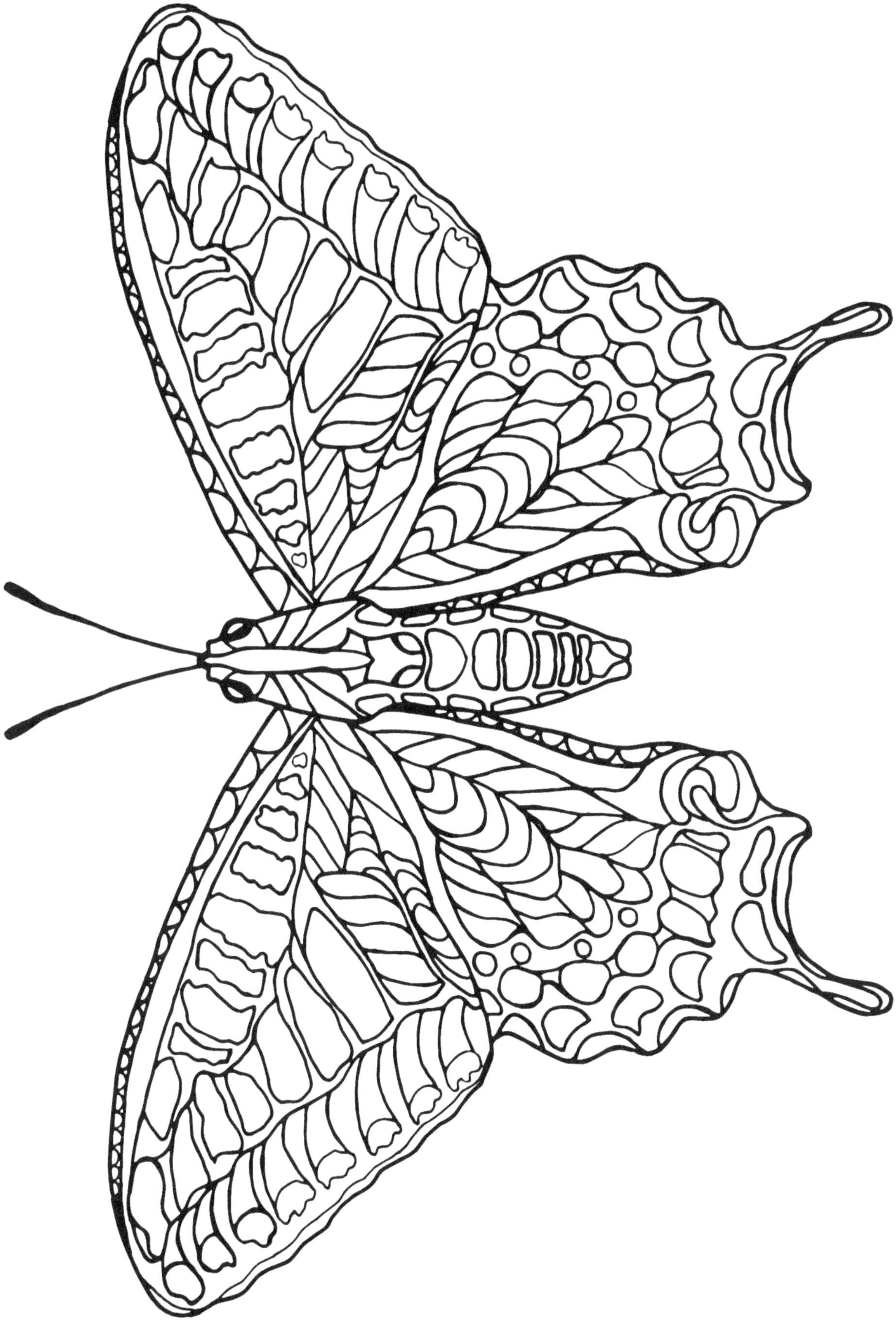

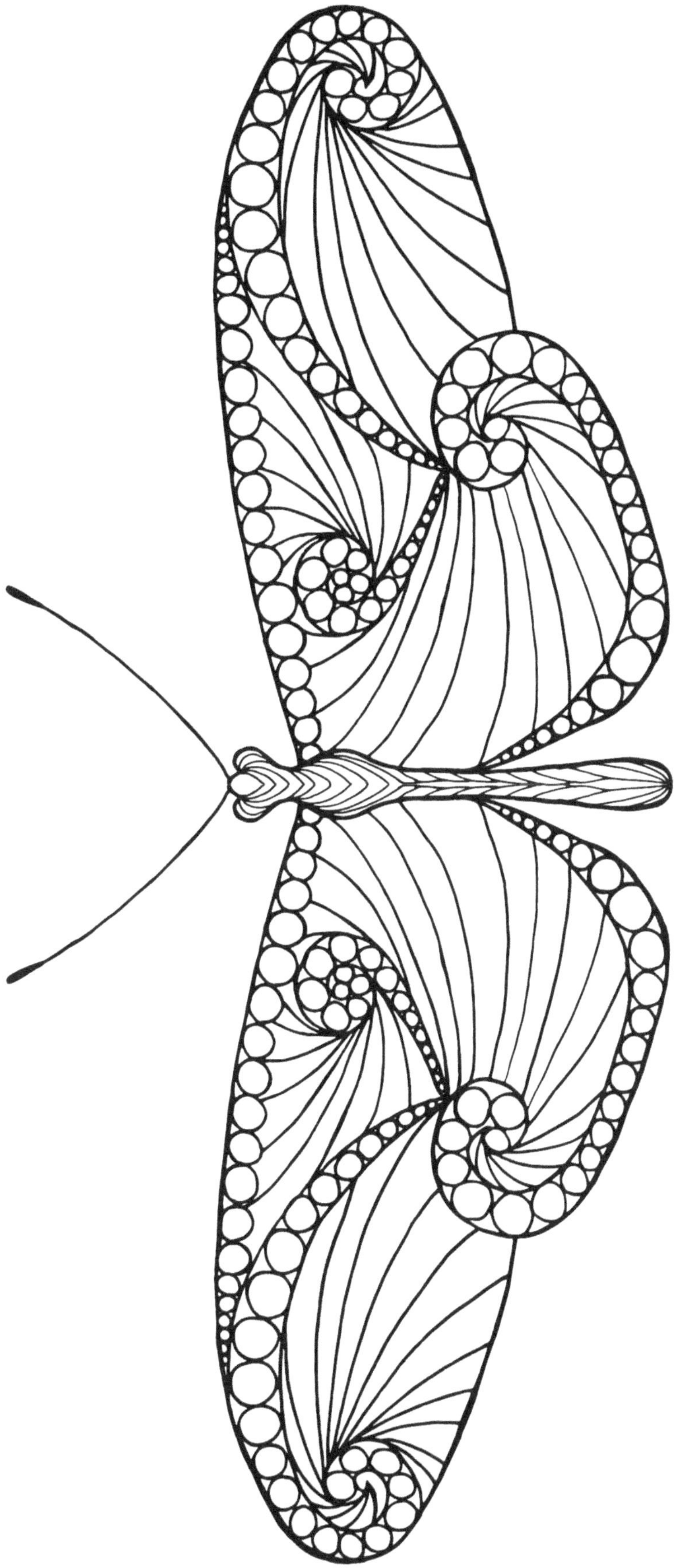

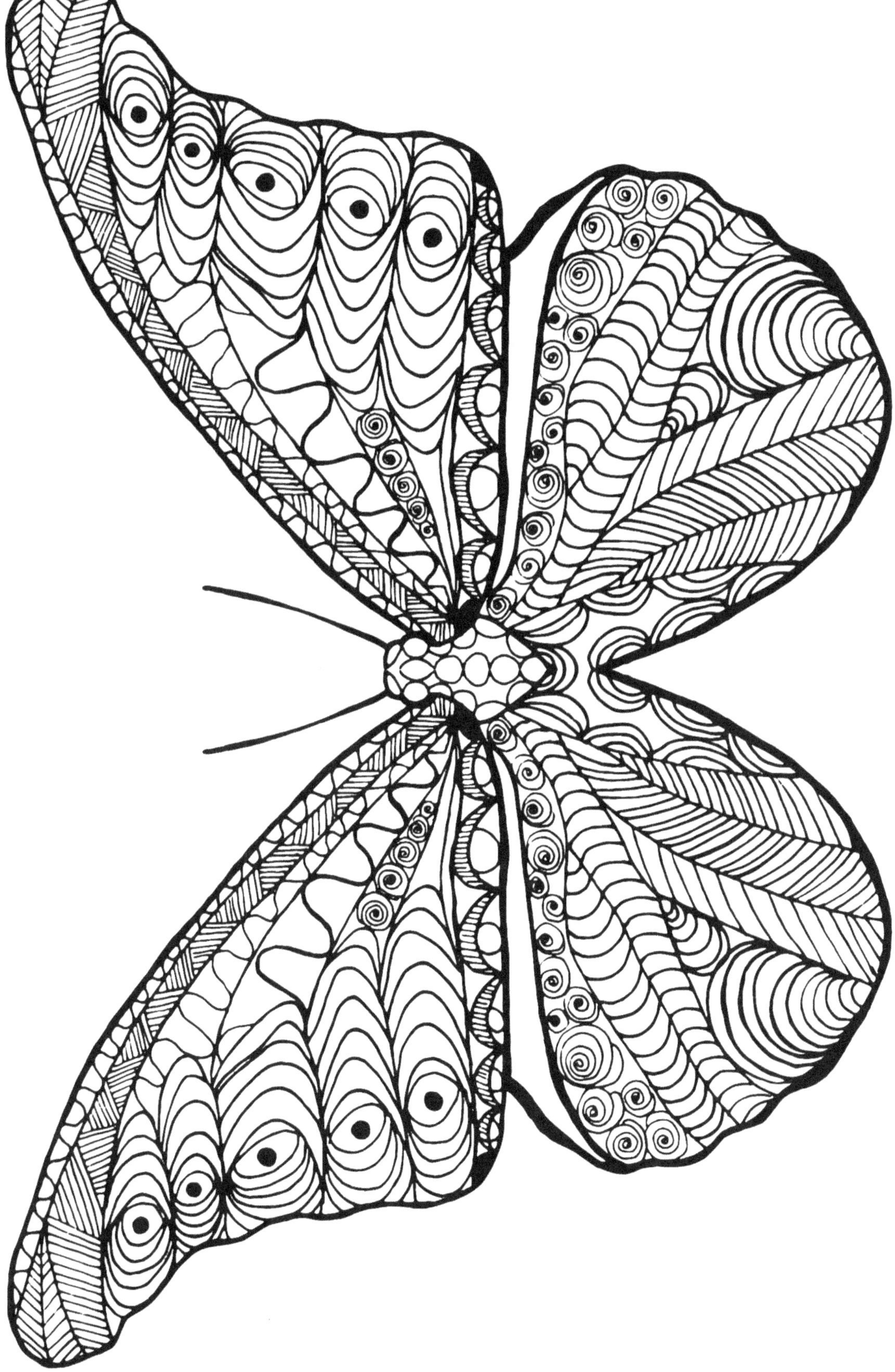

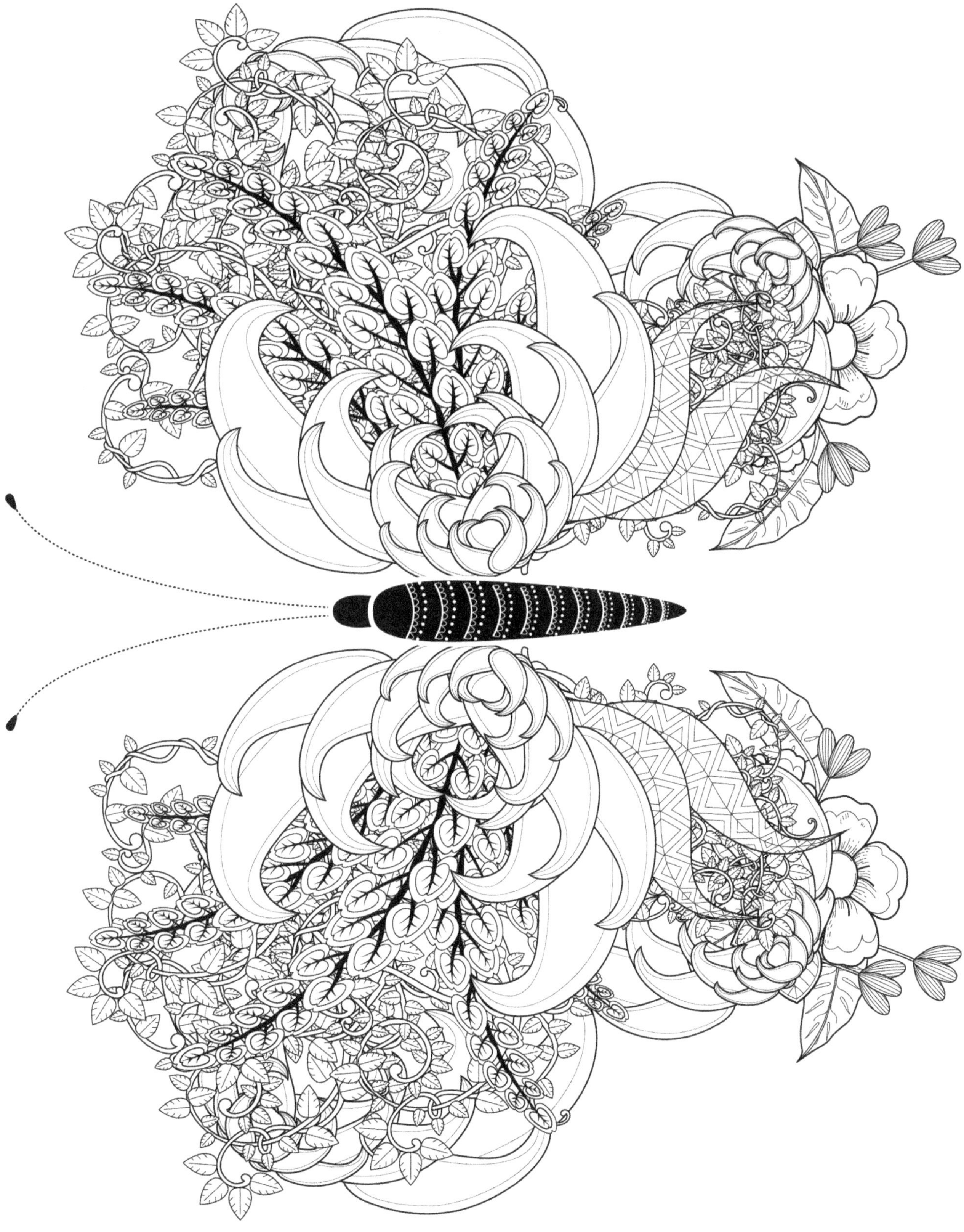

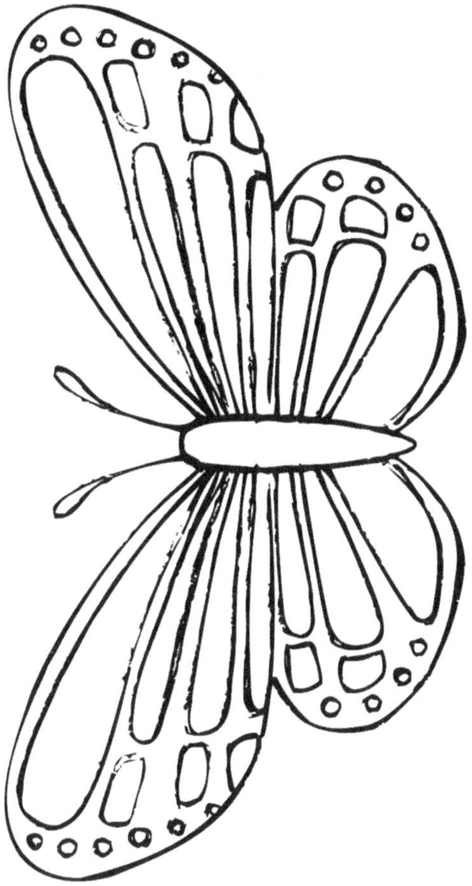

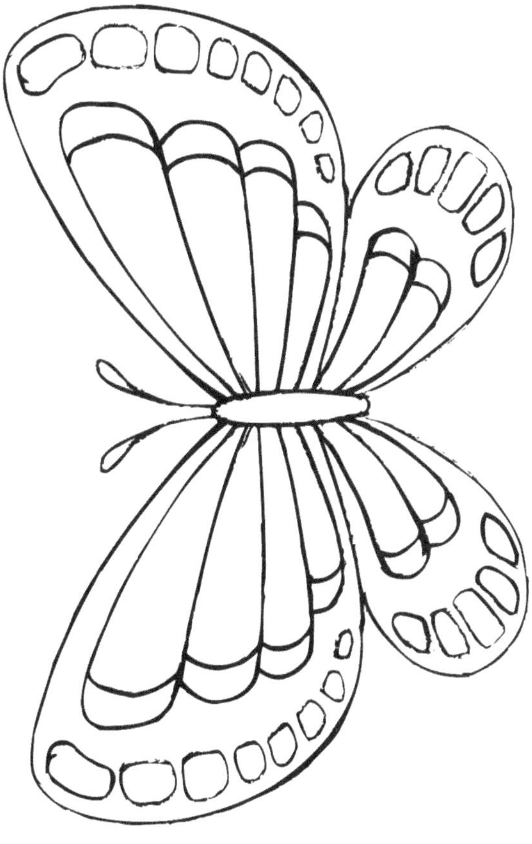

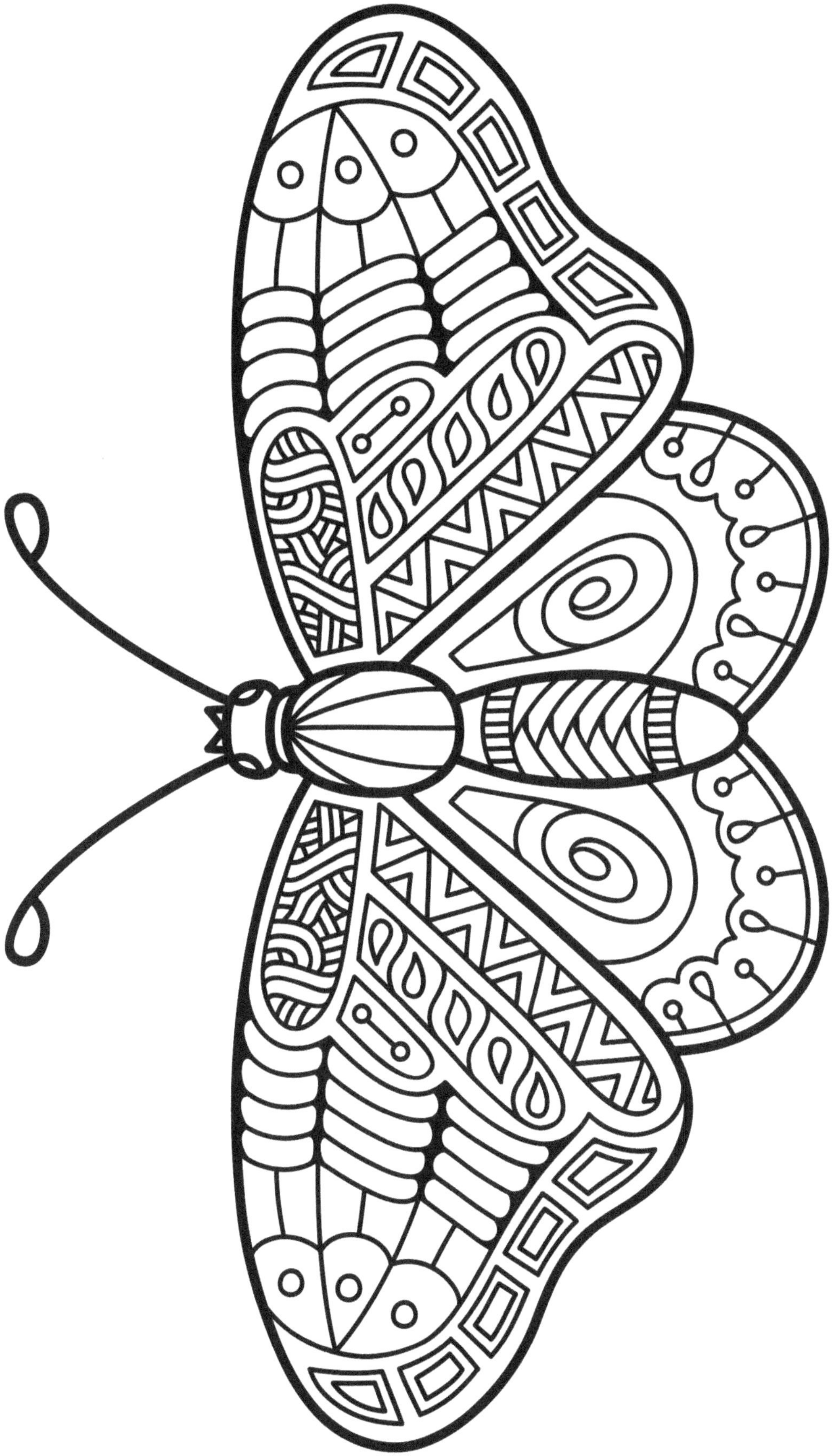

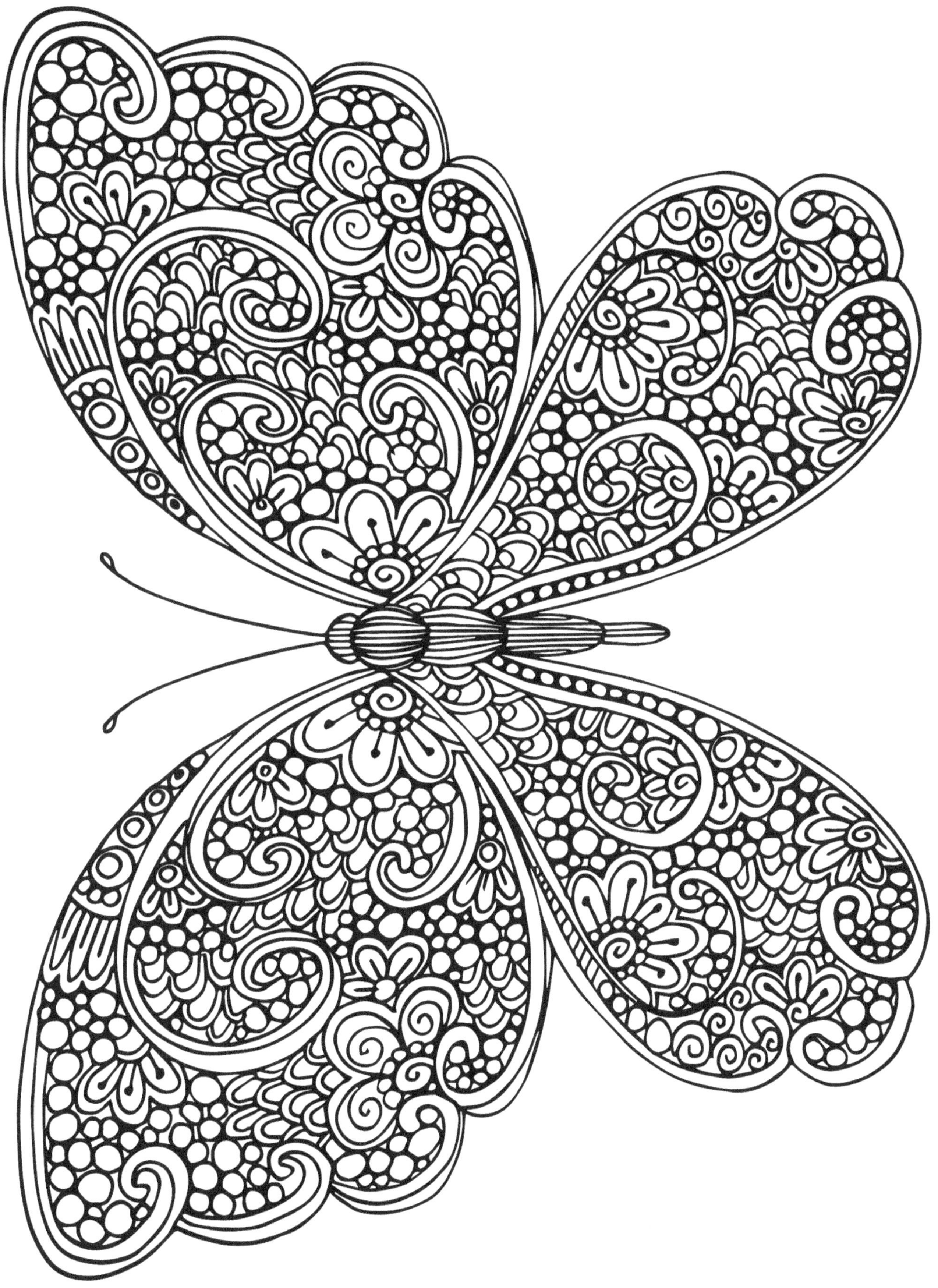

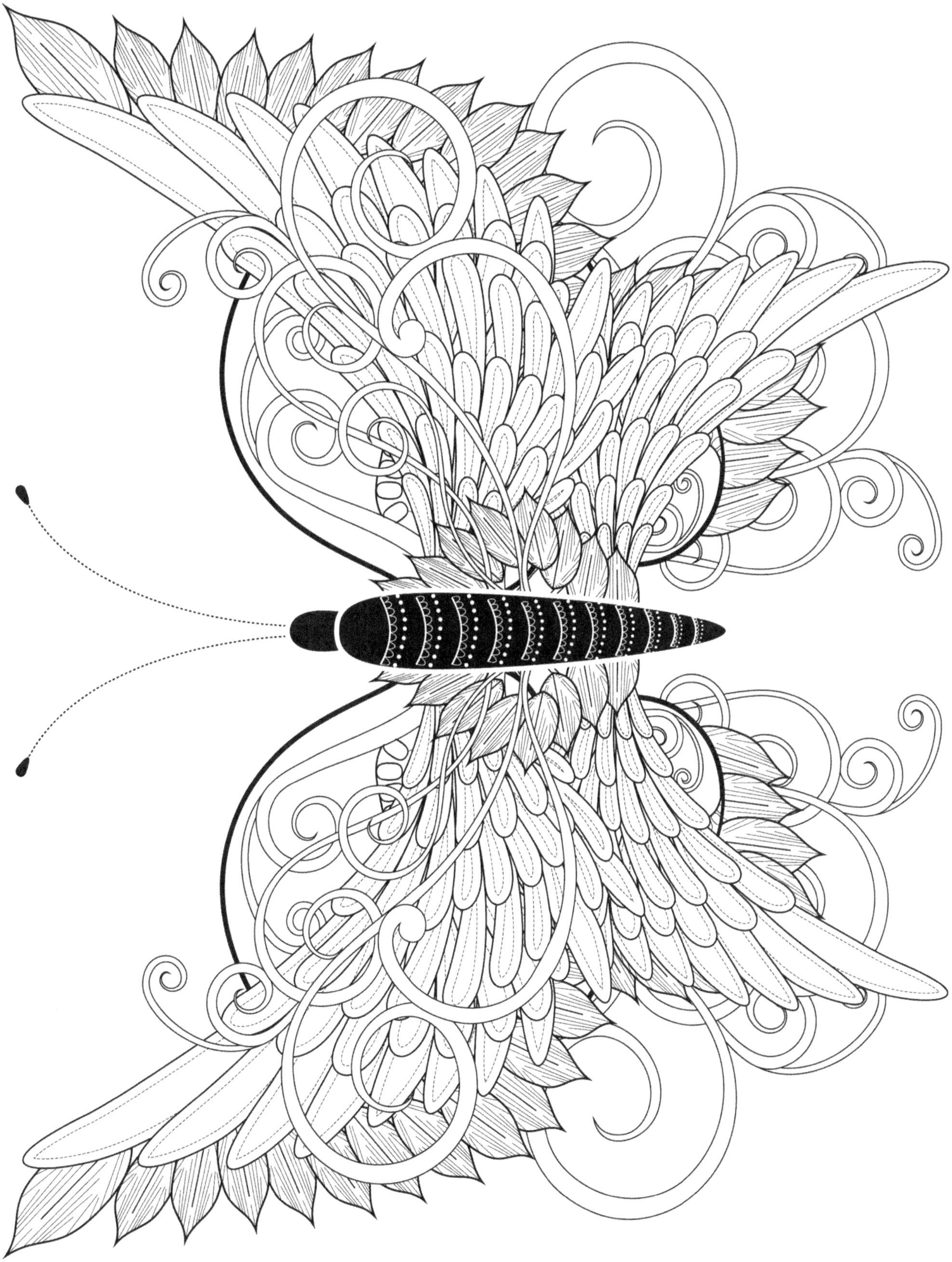

www.ingramcontent.com/pod-product-compliance
Lightning Source LLC
Chambersburg PA
CBHW081408280526
45788CB00009B/3027
* 9 7 8 1 5 2 3 2 5 2 9 8 5 *